A People in Focus Book

Sounding

THE **ALARM**

A Biography of Rachel Carson

Judith
Harlan

dP | DILLON PRESS, INC.
Minneapolis, Minnesota 55415

For my mother
who is also a woman of great heart and humor

Acknowledgments

Photographs have been reproduced through the courtesy of the Beinecke Rare Book and Manuscript Library, Yale University (pages 15, 61, 85, 93, 87); Chatham College (pages 33, 42); and the Ferdinand Hamburger, Jr., Archives, Johns Hopkins University (page 48). Additional photos by Erich Hartmann (cover, pages 6, 107), Shirley A. Briggs (pages 67, 77, 89, 119), and the Carson family (pages 11, 17, 21) are reproduced through the courtesy of the Rachel Carson Council.

Portions of Rachel Carson's letters are excerpted from *The House of Life* by Paul Brooks (pages 16, 18, 20, 21, 30-31, 33, 35, 71, 72, 75-76, 77, 78-80, 82, 86-88, 101, 111, 113, 116, 119, 208, 211, 213, 242, 265, 272, 314, 323, 326-327). ©1972 by Paul Brooks. Reprinted by permission of Houghton Mifflin Company.

Additional material has been reprinted by permission of Frances Collin, Trustee: "Rachel Carson's Early Years," by Wendy Wareham, *Carnegie* Magazine, November/December 1986 (pages 25, 28, 30, 33), ©1987 by Roger Christie; "A Battle in the Clouds," *St. Nicholas* Magazine, September 1918; and Rachel Carson's personal letters.

Library of Congress Cataloging-in-Publication Data

Harlan, Judith.
  Sounding the Alarm : a biography of Rachel Carson / Judith
Harlan.
    p.   cm. — (A People in focus book)
  Bibliography: p.
  Includes index.
  Summary: Traces the life and achievements of the biologist who
wrote about the sea and the dangers of pesticides.
  ISBN 0-87518-407-3

  1. Carson, Rachel, 1907-1964—Juvenile literature. 2. Ecolo-
gists—United States—Biography—Juvenile literature. [1. Carson, Rachel, 1907-1964. 2. Conservationists. 3. Biologists.]
I. Title.   II. Series..
  QH31.C33H37   1989
  574'.092'4—dc 19
  [B]
  [92]   88-35909
                                                        CIP
                                                        AC

Dillon Press, Inc., 242 Portland Avenue South
Minneapolis, Minnesota 55415

Printed in the United States of America
1 2 3 4 5 6 7 8 9 10 98 97 96 95 94 93 92 91 90 89

Contents

Chapter/One

A rather solitary child

Rachel had been walking and then crouching in the cold, Atlantic waters for more than an hour. She could no longer feel her toes, but this was a fact she had not noticed yet.

She was too busy watching a tiny seahorse as it lowered itself from the roof of a small cave. The seahorse, in turn, was watching its own reflection in the tidepool below it.

Rachel crouched down low on a narrow, ocean-side ledge so that she could peer closer into the seahorse's small, private cave. This was a "fairy pool," she later wrote, an "enchanted place on the threshold of the sea."

Rachel watched with the wonder of a small child seeing ocean life for the first time. Yet she was not a child. She was more than forty years old, a famous biologist, author of two books about the sea, and in the middle of writing a third.

At this point in her life, she still had many words to write. Less than ten years later, she would be the first popular scientist to warn Americans about the dangers of using certain chemicals. Though her books about the sea were beautiful and millions of people read them, Rachel Carson would not go down in history as an oceanography writer. She would be known as America's first ecologist.

She would spend her last years studying DDT (dichloro-diphenyl-trichloroethane) and other chemicals. Americans were using these chemicals to kill mosquitoes and also insects that attacked the crops grown on farms across the nation. Rachel would warn us to take care. Our wildlife, our fish, and even our own lives, she wrote, could be in danger.

Those days of alarm were still far in the future as Rachel crouched beside the cold tidepool and watched the seahorse watch himself. She was still concentrating then on the passion of her life—the plant and animal world of the sea.

Rachel Carson's love for the life forms that occupy the planet Earth can be traced back to her earliest childhood—back to the influence of her mother, Maria Frazier McLean Carson. "More than anyone else I know," Rachel once said about her mother, "she embodied Albert Schweitzer's 'reverence for life.'...Her love of life and of all living things was her outstanding quality."

All living creatures, even spiders and bugs, Maria Carson taught young Rachel, have value, each in its own way. While other mothers were swatting spiders and flying insects with rolled up newspapers, Rachel's mother was shooing them out the door. She felt they should be allowed to continue their short lives, as long as they did so on the other side, the outside, of her front door.

Through eyes filtered by this wealth of love for all things natural, young Rachel looked around at the world. Everything was new and exciting. Birds called from the woods, enticing Rachel off the back porch and across the yard to seek them out. Mysterious tracks left by hidden forest animals attracted her beyond the yard and into the woods. She followed them until they vanished, as mysteriously as they had appeared, into a crack between two rocks or into a bed of forest leaves. Rachel explored in every direction, through tree shadows and meadow sunlight, roaming the sixty-five-acre woods that surrounded her house. Through those first long, carefree summers of her life, Rachel's only companion was often her little dog, Candy.

"I was rather a solitary child," Rachel explained, "and spent a great deal of time in woods and beside streams, learning the birds and the insects and flowers." At other times, though, she walked alongside her mother, the two disappearing for long afternoons into the woods. Rachel learned to listen quietly for the rustlings of wild creatures. Tiny ones would hide under leaves and race off, helter-skelter, when she pushed their leaf roofs aside. Bigger ones would rush through the branches of trees overhead. Then at night, while she was inside the house, raccoons and oppossums would leave telltale tracks. In the morning, Rachel would discover that these nocturnal animals had been crossing the yard again, hunting through the night for their food.

The Carsons also kept farm animals, and if Rachel tired of chasing the shadows of wild animals, she could always find the family's domestic animals close at hand. She could walk up to the cows and pat them on the head, tickle the horse under the chin, or watch the pigs and chickens in the farmyard. Sometimes she also followed her mother as Maria Carson scattered cracked corn for the chickens. Rachel would toss a handful out, too. Then all

Holding a doll, Rachel stands in the yard next to her home in the Pennsylvania countryside.

the chuckling, feathered creatures would gather at her feet as well as at her mother's. A girl didn't have to be terribly old or grown up to be a big help at chicken-feeding time.

Rachel's home was in a private, wooded area, but it was by no means luxurious. The Carsons' house was small, just two rooms on the first floor and three small ones on the second. The kitchen was a lean-to affair attached to the side of the structure. A spring house, a small, outdoor enclosure through which an icy cold spring ran, served as the "refrigerator" for eggs, milk, and other foods. The house had no bathroom, just an outhouse. Living on this small farm could be rugged during the cold winter months—rugged yet always satisfyingly beautiful.

Rachel's father, Robert Warden Carson, had first brought the Carsons to this quiet Pennsylvania home. Buying the sixty-five acres near the small town of Springdale, located about eighteen miles from Pittsburgh, was to be just the beginning for Robert Carson. He hoped to make a great deal of money in the real estate business.

From Pittsburgh originally, Robert Carson was a quiet man who chose his words carefully. He was also something of an amateur singer. In 1894, when he met Rachel's mother, he was traveling and singing with a church quartet which performed in Maria's town of Washington, Pennsylvania.

Maria McLean, also a talented singer, was a member of the Washington Quintette Club. She was a schoolteacher, a job she enjoyed, and she played the piano. Her older sister, Ida, taught piano. Maria, her sister, and their mother had lived in Washington since Maria's father, a Presbyterian minister, had died.

When Maria married Robert Carson, she was forced to quit teaching because in those days most towns required teachers to be single. She turned her attention to starting a family. In 1897, Rachel's older sister, Marian, was born, followed by Rachel's brother, Robert, in 1899. Then the Carsons bought their land and moved to the countryside that would become Rachel's home, too.

Robert Carson hoped that one day he would be able to divide his new property into lots and make a large profit by selling them. While he waited for property values to rise and interest in his land to develop, he supported his family by selling insurance and other real estate, and by working as an electrical substation operator for the power company.

By the time Rachel was born, the family was well-settled onto their land. Rachel's brother,

Robert, was eight, and her sister, Marian, was ten.
When Rachel was six, both her brother and sister
were teenagers, and Rachel, the baby of the family, was the only child in a household of adults.
The center of much attention, she grew and devel-
oped into a confident young girl who shared her
father's quiet, reserved personality and care for the
spoken word.

Her mother, though, was her most constant
guide and friend. Maria Carson, somewhat separated from the activity of the nearest town, spent
most of her time with her family.

In the early 1900s, without televisions or radios
to entertain them, families throughout the world
entertained themselves. Rachel's mother still sang,
and so did Rachel's father, at least in the living
room of their own home. During the quiet evenings
after dinner, Maria Carson would often sit down at
the piano and lead the Carson family quintet, har-
monizing to the songs of the day. At other times, the
family would gather around Maria Carson while she
read aloud. They would hear stories of far-off
adventures—stories that would transport Rachel to
the decks of a ship, to a castle in Europe, or even to
an Indian camp before the American Revolution.

Maria Carson had been reading to Rachel ever
since Rachel could remember, and sometime during

*Sitting on her mother's lap, Rachel poses for a family portrait with her
sister, Marian (left), and her brother, Robert (right).*

those early childhood days Rachel had decided she
would be a writer when she grew up. "I have no
idea why," she said years later. "I suppose I must
have realized someone wrote the books and thought
it would be fun to make up stories, too." She did
not know it when she was a child, but she would
write wonderful books about the ocean. Already,
she was fascinated by the sea.

Her enthusiasm for the ocean and all of its mysterious unknowns was not dampened by the fact
that the Carsons lived far from the sea. Even at
an early age, Rachel imagined what the ocean was
like. She often picked up the big, ocean conch shell
that her mother kept on the living room table. She
would put it close to her ear and listen to its roar.
Was this the ocean? Was this the way the surf
sounded as it pounded against coastal rocks? The
ocean's spirit, captured in the conch's pink spiral,
was whispering into Rachel's ear. It was a compell-
ing, husky voice.

Rachel would one day see the ocean, but meanwhile, she concentrated on becoming a writer. By
the time she was eight years old, she was writing
poetry. Her poems were short and childlike, but
what mattered most to Rachel was that they were
warmly received by her family and teachers. She
continued to write them.

Rachel reads a book to her dog, Candy. She was often alone and imagined what faraway places such as the ocean might be like.

In school Rachel studied hard and earned high grades. She enjoyed learning, and almost always completed her homework and paid attention in class. Her teachers remembered her as a bright, quiet student, but they worried about the number of days she was absent.

Rachel's mother was very protective of her third and last child. She feared that one of the numerous contagious diseases that ran through the community during the school year would take Rachel from her.

Diseases that are now controlled were, in Rachel's childhood, often killers. Her grandfather had died from tuberculosis when he was just forty years old. And polio swept through the region in epidemic proportions in 1916 when Rachel was nine. The only vaccine available at the time was one for smallpox. Because there was no preventive medicine, many children caught diphtheria, whooping cough, the measles, and the mumps. They came down with influenza, too, and it could be a serious illness. With no antibiotics to combat complications that can develop when the system is weakened by the flu, the virus could signal the beginning of severe illness. It could even be fatal. In 1918 and 1919, when Rachel was eleven, more than 500,000 people in the United States died from the "Spanish Influenza."

Rachel's mother was taking no chances. At the first sign of any contagious diseases in the area, she would keep Rachel home from school. She also kept her home when the weather was particularly stormy or severely cold. Maria Carson knew that a morning chill that lasted through the school day, then was followed by a long, cold walk home at night, could expose Rachel to a number of illnesses, many of them fatal. Any thoughts of picking Rachel up at school in the family horse-and-buggy would usually have to be put aside. The farm roads leading from the Carson land into town would become unusable for much of the winter. And in later years, when the Carsons had a car, they would put it away in the barn for the entire winter because the roads became so rutted and impassable.

Rachel's schoolwork, though, did not suffer. She was always ready with the right answers, her teachers reported, even after just returning from a long absence. She had no difficulty keeping up because her mother tutored her during these periods.

At home, Rachel was secure. Diseases that swept through the city seldom reached the Carson farm. Even the war—World War I—must have seemed far away at first.

Rachel was seven in 1914 when the assassination of Archduke Franz Ferdinand of Austria started the conflict. At first the United States remained neutral, believing that this was Europe's war. While the Central Powers (Germany, Austria-Hungary, and Turkey) declared war on the Allied Powers (Britain, France, Russia, and later Italy and the United States), the United States remained on the sidelines, concerned with other events. The Panama Canal opened. Automobiles were replacing the horse-and-buggy, and progress was the talk of the day.

In May 1915, a German submarine sank the *Lusitania*, a British passenger ship, killing 1,200 passengers. Of these, 128 were Americans. Even then, the United States remained neutral. Over the next two years, however, the United States's neutral policy gradually changed. The war expanded, and it was no longer possible to believe that it was of no concern at home.

On April 6, 1917, the United States declared war on Germany. On June 5, almost 10 million Americans between the ages of twenty-one and thirty-one registered for the military draft. Many more volunteered to serve in the armed forces.

Rachel, ten years old, watched her eighteen-year-old brother join the U.S. Army Aviation Service and go off to Texas to train for battle. It was a sad day for the Carsons, but a proud day, too. Robert's letters brought news to the family and new insights for young Rachel. The war was serious business. Her brother was a part of it, and so were the thousands of other young men who entered the armed forces. President Woodrow Wilson assured the country that this was a "war to end war," a war to make the world safe for democracy.

Rachel's favorite publication, the *St. Nicholas Magazine*, encouraged its young readers to do what they could to help the American soldiers overseas. One group of the magazine's young readers reported that they each gave up something new—a

During World War I, Rachel stands next to Robert, dressed in his U.S. Army Aviation service uniform, and Marian.

hat, a pair of gloves, a new dress—and contributed the money to the U.S. government instead. Children, men, and women all across the country were doing what they could to help. Almost everyone knew someone or had someone in the family who was going off to war. *St. Nicholas Magazine* asked its young readers to write a short article about fighter pilots and their bravery. The best articles would be published in the magazine's monthly "St. Nicholas League" section.

This was a part of the magazine that had been fascinating Rachel for some time. It consisted of a few pages of children's contributions, and it announced prizes awarded for poetry, prose, photography, drawings, and puzzles. Each month the best contributions won gold and silver badges. Rachel read the short stories and essays written by children her own age, her eyes lingering on the bylines (names) of the young authors. What would her name look like if it were on those pages?

In September 1918, when Rachel was ten, she found out. Her essay, "A Battle in the Clouds," won a spot on *St. Nicholas Magazine*'s printed pages. What's more, her essay won the silver badge that month. She wrote about a pilot, a story she had heard from her brother. This is how it appeared in the magazine.

A BATTLE IN THE CLOUDS

By Rachel L. Carson (Age 10)
Silver Badge

This is a story about a famous aviator who was in the Royal Flying Corps until he was killed in this country instructing other men. The main facts of this story were told to me by my brother, who is a soldier. The aviator had been several years in France. One day, when he and one of his companions were flying, a German plane suddenly burst upon them from behind a cloud. The two planes began firing, and the anti-aircraft guns of the Allies and Germans began firing. For a while, neither plane was injured, but soon the German plane began to fall, for the aviator was shot. But it was too late, for the damage had already been done, as part of one wing of the Canadian aviator's plane had been shot away. The plane wavered, and he knew that if something was not done promptly, the plane would fall. He saw that there was only one thing to do, and he did it quickly. He crawled out along the wing, inch by inch, until he reached the end. He then hung from the end of the wing, his weight making the plane balance properly. The Germans saw him, but could not but respect and admire the daring and courage of the aviators, and did not fire until the plane landed safely. The aviator was killed a few months ago in a training-camp in this country, and, in my opinion, the Allies, by his death, lost a brave and daring soldier.

For her contribution, Rachel received ten dollars, a large sum for a young girl in 1918, and her first professional pay.

"I doubt that any royalty check of recent years has given me as great joy as the notice of that award," Rachel wrote years later after she had become a famous biologist and author. "Perhaps that early experience of seeing my work in print played its part in fostering my childhood dream of becoming a writer."

Chapter/Two

Rachel's like the midday sun

Rachel's stories were to appear at least three more times in St. *Nicholas Magazine*, with "Honor Member" written below her name. In 1919, when she was eleven, one of her stories won the magazine's gold badge. Another one, called "A Story of the Sea," began with this passage:

> George Markham shivered and drew his coat closer around him. It was a very cold night, and he was wet to the skin with spray. His watch was to last two hours, and only one hour had elapsed since he had left his bunk and come up to the cold, windy deck.

Rachel was already imagining what the sea was like in this story, which describes an American warship's encounter with a submarine during World War I.

As the war came to an end, life on the Carson family farm was changing. Rachel's sister, Marian, had married when Rachel was in grammar school and by this time had two daughters, Marjorie and Virginia. Her father worked as an insurance agent for the Great American Insurance Company of New York, and still hoped to divide the family's farm into small lots that could be sold for a large sum of money. He also continued to sell apples from the orchard for fifty cents a bushel to anyone who wanted to go in and pick them.

The nearby town was changing, too. In 1910, when Rachel was three, Springdale had had a population of 1,199. Now, as she was entering high school, that population had grown to almost 3,000. The property next door to the Carsons had been bought by a glass factory, and workers were digging great holes into the sand there.

Meanwhile, Rachel was growing into a fine young woman. Her hair was brown, her skin fair, and her eyes blue. She was a hard worker at school and enjoyed a contented family life at home.

Her mother, Maria, gave piano lessons for fifty cents a lesson on the old upright piano that sat in the Carsons' downstairs front room. Since young ladies of the era were encouraged to be accomplished in piano and often in singing as well, Maria had no trouble finding young students. She sold them their sheet music and scale exercise charts, too, and was apparently a strict taskmaster. When they missed one of their weekly lessons, the students were expected to make it up.

After the lessons, when the Carson family was alone again, Maria would still play for her family. Some of the songs she played were ones she wrote herself. Besides reading, music was Maria Carson's first love. She wrote it, studied it, and played it as often as she could.

Rachel completed ninth and tenth grades at Springdale High School (a two-year institution). Then she went on to Parnassus High School for the eleventh and twelfth grades. Because Rachel was a good student, her teachers often asked her to read her compositions in class. And the other students grew accustomed to seeing Rachel standing in front of the class reading a paper.

Yet, even though Rachel impressed her teachers, she did not make many friends among her schoolmates. Since she commuted to the school from Springdale, she had to leave right after classes to ride home on a streetcar. That meant she couldn't stay late and participate in afterschool clubs, sports, or informal get-togethers with the others. While her friends were planning where they would meet after classes, what they would wear, what the club's activities would be, and all the other exciting events of high school life, Rachel would be gathering her books, putting on her coat, and checking through her wallet for her streetcar token.

Years later her classmates remembered her as a solitary girl. While her teachers saw her as studious, her classmates called her bookish. She was different, but she was not unliked. An inscription in her yearbook beside her photo reads:

> Rachel's like the mid-day sun
> Always very bright
> Never stops studying
> 'Til she gets it right.

Rachel was facing some serious decisions about her life. Her mother and father were determined that she would go to college, and she wanted to go, too. But where was the money to come from? During her senior year, Rachel and her mother researched the possibilities.

One college that appealed to both Rachel and her mother was Pennsylvania College for Women (the name was changed to Chatham College in 1955). It was small, had a good academic reputation, and Rachel's mother liked its atmosphere. The college was built on a bluff overlooking Pittsburgh.

Its lawns were well-tended, its trees were stately, and its walls were ivy-covered.

But it was costly. Tuition and expenses would run from $800 to $1,000 per year, a great deal of money for a family that sold piano lessons for fifty cents an hour and apples for fifty cents a bushel. Still, the Carsons had their land, and Robert Carson had already offered sixteen lots to the Springdale School District at a price of $11,000. But the district hesitated, and then in 1925 finally rejected the offer.

In the end, Rachel's outstanding school record came to her rescue. She won a scholarship to attend the college. The amount of the award was only $100, but the college's president, Cora Helen Coolidge, and its dean, Mary Marks, were impressed by Rachel. Together, they gathered up a special, unofficial scholarship fund for her, money donated privately from a few wealthy friends of the college. Even with outside help, though, Rachel continued to have problems paying for tuition and living expenses throughout her college years. Eventually she went into debt to the college and signed over some of her land to them as payment.

Nevertheless, she was now officially a college student. Her major was English, and she was determined to study hard and learn well. In one of her first college essays, titled "Who I am and Why I

Came to PCW (Pennsylvania College for Women)," Rachel described herself as "a girl of eighteen years, a Presbyterian, Scotch-Irish by ancestry..." And, she wrote, "...[I am] intensely fond of anything pertaining to outdoors and athletics. I am seldom happier than when I am before a glowing campfire with the open sky above my head. I love all the beautiful things of nature, and the wild creatures are my friends."

Life at PCW was unlike anything Rachel had ever experienced before. She was living away from her family for the first time, and she was surrounded by young women her own age, many of them from wealthy families. Parties, dances, dates— these were the subjects of conversations in the halls after classes during the last few years of the Roaring Twenties. Dances were energetic, hemlines were high, and young women were experimenting with smoking. Rachel, her college friend Dorothy Seif explained, "didn't waste her time sitting chatting and smoking with the girls." But she was enthusiastic about sports and played field hockey, basketball, and softball, and she was always busy with essays, assignments, and reading.

PCW trained many of its students to become teachers, one of the few professions open to women in the 1920s. Other young women were there to complete their educations and prepare for their roles as wives and mothers. A few students at PCW would go on to graduate study. Rachel was one of these.

She stood out immediately from her fellow students because she was studious, reserved, and quite a bit less wealthy than most of them. To help pay expenses, her mother worked extra hours teaching piano lessons, clerking at a local store, and selling chickens from the farm. Rachel's father took whatever jobs he could find, too. In addition to her naturally hard-working nature, Rachel felt a duty to her family and the other people helping her to do well in her studies.

Her classmates later remembered that Rachel seldom went on dates or to school dances and parties. Dorothy Seif, who like Rachel was not as rich as most PCW students, recalled that the other young women always seemed to have beautiful clothes. They had extra money to spend on stockings, purses, and party clothes. Rachel did not.

Her mother visited often, though, bringing clothes she had made for Rachel, and baskets of cookies. Maria Carson sometimes stayed to type papers for her daughter, and Rachel went home for weekends as often as she could.

Rachel spent a great deal of time studying.

When she wasn't studying, she was working on school projects. She became a reporter for PCW's paper, the *Arrow*, when she was a freshman. By the end of that year, her circle of friends and acquaintances had slowly grown to include other girls who, like her, were interested in English and in writing. One of Rachel's short stories, "The Master of the Ship's Light," was published in the "Englicode," a special literary supplement to the paper printed at the end of the school year.

In her sophomore year, Rachel wrote a story that won the annual English prize. She joined the yearbook staff, and played goalie for her field hockey team. Money continued to be a constant problem for her. Usually, she didn't have the extra fifteen cents it took to stop for a soda with her teammates after field hockey practice.

One of her classmates, Helen Myers, recalled going home with Rachel for a weekend on the Carson farm. Mr. Carson was out of town, and Rachel's brother and sister were both living on their own by then. Myers remembered that she slept in a bed in the main downstairs room. The house was "poor looking," she said. "[Rachel's] mother had sold all of the good china, the good things, to pay for Rachel's tuition." Maria Carson sold everything but the piano, reported Dorothy Seif. She would

Rachel (top row, second from right) *with the members of her college field hockey team.*

have sold that, too, but she needed it to give piano lessons.

Though times were tough financially, Rachel's schoolwork was exciting. In her sophomore year she enrolled in a class that would change the course of her life. She had always thought she would study English, write great stories and novels, and earn her living as an author. A required course in biology and a dedicated teacher's contagious enthusiasm changed that plan.

Mary Scott Skinker was the biology professor, and her course was the first that Rachel had ever taken in the subject. In the classroom and the

laboratory with Professor Skinker's class, Rachel
discovered she could study the outdoors, animals,
wildlife—all "the beautiful things of nature" she
had said she loved so much. For the first time in her
life, she was studying the wildlife she had grown up
watching on the Carson farm. Here were the expla-
nations for the creatures under the leaves and the
animals that made the footprints that marched by
her house at night.

Professor Skinker's class was not easy. She required textbook work and laboratory experiments.
Contrary to the current belief of her day, she believed that young women could learn science as well
as men could. Her courses were technical and demanding. They built the foundations students needed to go on to graduate study.

The young teacher was at odds with Cora Coolidge, president of the college, who believed the
courses should be less demanding. Coolidge argued
that women should not be encouraged to enter the
sciences because there were limited opportunities
for them in those occupations. Other than teaching
posts, women could expect few jobs to be open to
them. Skinker wanted more science classes, while
Cora Coolidge wanted fewer.

In the midst of this debate, during her junior
year, Rachel Carson stunned the officials at PCW

by announcing that she was changing her major. She was giving up English, which everyone thought offered great career opportunities for her as a writer. Rachel had ideas of her own. To her friend, Mary Frye, Rachel wrote: "I have something very exciting to tell you. Get a big breath, Mary! Here goes; I've changed my major. To what? Biology, of course. Miss Skinker hasn't recovered from the shock yet. She says after this nothing will ever surprise her."

Chapter/Three

For the mighty wind arises, roaring seaward, and I go

"I do love to say I'm majoring in Biology," Rachel wrote to Mary Frye, "but you ought to see the reactions I get. I've gotten bawled out and called all sorts of blankety-blank names so much that it's beginning to get monotonous. That's all from the girls of course—the teachers have been lovely. But nobody seems to understand why I'd give up English for Biology."

The president of the college tried to persuade Rachel to change her decision. Not only would a life in biology waste Rachel's writing talent, Cora Coolidge argued, but it would be physically demanding, possibly too much so for Rachel. Coolidge also pointed out that very few females had ever been successful in the field. In 1928, biology and most of the other sciences were still a man's world.

Rachel would not change her mind. With just a year and a half to go before graduation, she began to work harder than ever. She had science classes to make up, most of them including laboratory time. She continued to work on the school newspaper and yearbook, and to play on the hockey team.

Rachel also continued to excel in her English courses. For one English assignment, she and her classmates were asked to write a triolet, which is an eight-line poem based on two rhymes. The graceful rhythm of the poem Rachel wrote and read to the class astonished her classmates. No one expected a college assignment to be so lovely.

> Butterfly poised on a thistle's down
> Lend me your wings for a summer's day.
> What care I for a kingly crown
> Butterfly poised on a thistle's down
> When I might wear your gossamer gown
> And sit enthroned on an orchid spray?
> Butterfly poised on a thistle's down
> Lend me your wings for a summer's day.

The triolet was published in both the school's newspaper and its yearbook.

Though Rachel spent long hours working in the science laboratory and was a devoted student, another, humorous side of her personality began to show during these months of hard work. Rachel loved a good prank, one that was well played and hurt no one.

Rachel's friend and science classmate, Dorothy Seif, recalled a funny incident that took place late one evening while the two girls worked in the science laboratory. Seif pointed out that the lab's alcohol supply was disappearing much more quickly than it should. This was during Prohibition, a period when alcoholic beverages were prohibited by law. The two girls concluded that someone was dipping into the lab's alcohol supply for non-scientific purposes. The next time they met in the lab, Rachel had some red food coloring with her. She dropped a squirt of it into the bottle, enough to turn the alcohol pink, slapped a skull and crossbones (poison) label on the container, and put the bottle back on the shelf. After that, Seif said, the alcohol supply stopped disappearing.

Science and the outdoors were blending together in Rachel's studies. She already shared her love of the outdoors with her mother, and now she began to share her scientific explorations with her, too. Dorothy Seif went on one afternoon outing with Rachel and Maria Carson, and she recalled that day. "Mrs. Carson was wearing an old housedress when we met her downtown," said Seif. "She had on old ugly shoes, her hair was pulled straight back and she was carrying a basket [of lunch] on her arm."

Yet Mrs. Carson "in her cotton dress," Seif recalled, was an impressive lady. "She began to discuss some things with us," Seif added, "and I realized that she was aware of everything that Rachel was doing. She was the one who had trained Rachel in the sense of wonder—to observe all the animals and plants and to identify them....She was a brilliant woman," Seif concluded, and "she knew her daughter was talented even then."

In her junior year at PCW, Rachel joined the other girls in one of the year's greatest social events, the prom. Her friend Helen Myers coaxed her into going. Helen's date brought a friend along for Rachel.

"It was so pretty," Rachel wrote to Mary Frye about the prom. "They had very dim lighting most of the time, and kept flashing green and lavender and yellow lights across the ballroom. A trifle hard on the eyes, but indescribably pretty on the glass chandeliers and the mirror walls."

The prom had been beautiful, and Rachel's date had been lovely. In fact, she went to a couple of football games with this young man after her prom night. But her concentration was not on this

social side of life, but on her career. She was
already thinking ahead to what she would do
after she graduated. "I'm going to go right on
and get my Master's degree," she explained in
a letter to Mary Frye.

In the summer between her junior and senior
year, Rachel tutored students and also took care of
her two nieces. "My sister went to the hospital,"
Rachel wrote to a friend that summer, "and I have
been getting my share of housekeeping and taking
care of her two youngsters." Thankfully, though,
Rachel wrote, "She is getting along pretty well and
will be home next week." Then, with typical good
humor, Rachel added: "Meanwhile, I'm earning
credits towards a home economics certificate..."

Completely caught up in her new subject, biology, Rachel wrote to Mary Frye that she and a
classmate were going to catch a few turtles in August. "I want to work on their brains next winter,"
she reported.

Also, she spent some time scooping waters out
of a pond in her area and then studying it. "[Profes-
sor Skinker] asked me to send her some stagnant
water from pools around here," she explained. "I
had a great time getting it, and then was afraid to
send it to her before I could be sure there were
some protozoans in it. So our doctor let me use his

microscope and I had lots of fun. But I didn't recognize a thing except Colpoda and Paramecia! I'm afraid I'll never be a protozoologist."

Yet Rachel was determined to be a biologist. She thought of transferring to The Johns Hopkins University for her senior year. Professor Skinker was on sabbatical from PCW for a year of study there. Rachel would have liked to continue studying with this teacher, and The Johns Hopkins University was known for the excellence of its biology department. But it wasn't to be. "I still haven't any idea what I'm going to do next year," she later wrote to Mary. "It looks very much as though I'll stay here."

Rachel's senior year of college came quickly. She was already in debt to the college for $613.85, but it was money well spent. She had a new focus to her life—biology—and she had learned a great deal about literature and writing, too. Somehow she found some spare time in her senior year to write poetry of her own. She quietly sent some of her poems to national magazines, but she wasn't published yet. Instead, she collected a large assortment of rejection slips.

Her last years of college were times of success, as well as times of failure. Rachel was learning to cope with both. It was an exciting, intense time, too.

Rachel Carson during the time she attended the Pennsylvania College for Women.

Years later, she looked back on those days and remembered a single night that helped shape her life. "On a night when rain and wind beat against the windows of my college dormitory room, a line from *Locksley Hall* [a poem by A.L. Tennyson] burned itself in my mind—*For the mighty wind arises, roaring seaward, and I go.*

"I can still remember my intense emotional response as that line spoke to something within me, seeming to tell me that my own path led to the sea—which then I had never seen—and that my own destiny was somehow linked with the sea..."

Rachel was nearing the end of her college career. Her teachers would remember her for her scholastic abilities, and some of her friends would remember her that way, too. Many more, though, would probably recall the day Rachel supplied a goat as a mascot for her field hockey team. The goat freed itself and ran onto the field among the girls, delighting them all.

Rachel had fun with her classmates, but she also worked hard. She was not content simply to study the books and do well in the subjects her college offered. She sought out experts and information outside the college, and spent many hours at the Carnegie Museum of Natural History and the Carnegie Library talking to curators there. She also asked for information and advice from science professors at the University of Pittsburgh.

The studying and hard work were rewarded in June 1929, when Rachel graduated from PCW with highest honors for academic achievement. Mary Skinker recommended her for a summer scholarship at the Woods Hole Marine Biological Laboratory. Rachel also won a one-year scholarship for graduate study in zoology at The Johns Hopkins University. She may have just graduated from college, but her real studying was only just beginning.

Rachel had never seen the ocean. She had read about it, studied it, and imagined it. Finally, the summer after graduating from PCW, she saw it for the very first time.

The sea was breathtaking. And, even more exciting for Rachel, she was studying it firsthand. She was at Woods Hole, Massachusetts, at one of the foremost scientific research facilities in the country.

Rachel shared a rented room with Mary Frye, her college laboratory partner. At work she had her own lab table and her own research assignment. "My room is in the Apartment House and is very comfortably furnished, even to hot and cold running water," she wrote to Dorothy. "My table is in the lab just across the street. There are about four others working in the same room. One's mail is delivered to his laboratory table!"

Rachel spent many long, happy hours in the Woods Hole Library doing research, and she spent many more simply absorbing the look and feel of the immense ocean that spread out before her. It was an exciting spectacle. "I could see the racing tidal currents pouring through the 'Hole' or watch the waves breaking at Nobska Point after a storm," she later said, "and there I first became really aware of the unseen ocean currents."

Her summer had its share of calm days and activities, too. During off-hours, she and the other young researchers often sat out in the sun. Rachel would bring pen and paper down to the beach and write letters there, while sunbathing with Mary Frye. She reported to Dorothy Seif: "I've completely despaired of ever getting brown; experts have shaken their heads over me and pronounced me just not that kind! However, I am getting sort of weathered looking, besides growing a crop of freckles!"

All too soon, the summer was over, and Rachel and Mary separated. Rachel was on her way to The Johns Hopkins University in Baltimore, Maryland. On the way, she stopped in Washington, D.C., at the U.S. Bureau of Fisheries for an interview with Elmer Higgins, head of the Division of Scientific

Inquiry. She was there to ask for Higgins's advice. What course of study would he recommend for a young scientist attending Johns Hopkins? What opportunities were there in the field? Throughout her life Rachel believed in the value of consulting experts. She would continue to do so for all her research projects and books.

The year was 1930, and the Great Depression brought hard times to people across the nation and the world. Many factories closed, workers were fired, and there were few or no jobs to be had anywhere. Charity organizations handed out bowls of soup and bread, and lines for these meager meals stretched for blocks.

Rachel may have felt fortunate to be studying at Johns Hopkins while around her the country toiled and stumbled. And yet, she also knew that her years of studying and responsible work had made it possible for her to be where she was. The help and dedication of her mother, too, had been invaluable.

Rachel's new course of study required long hours of research and laboratory work. She studied under H.S. Jennings and Raymond Pearl, and served as lab assistant to Pearl. She wrote a detailed research thesis, a project that required painfully long hours over a microscope and equally long hours in the library.

Rachel's mother and father, both of them more than sixty years old by then, moved to Baltimore when Rachel started school. Even Rachel's brother, Robert Jr., came home to live for a while during these Depression years. He was working as a radio repair estimator.

Rachel took a job as part-time assistant in zoology at the University of Maryland. This, in addition to her duties as Pearl's assistant and her studies, kept her running. She didn't stop during summer vacation. During those summer months she worked as a teaching assistant in biology for Johns Hopkins's summer sessions.

In 1932, Rachel received her master's degree in zoology from Johns Hopkins. She had completed her formal education and was ready to face the world of science. At first, Rachel found few job opportunities. Jobs were hard to find in any field, and Rachel was entering one that traditionally belonged to men.

Rachel continued to work as a teaching assistant in the summers at Johns Hopkins and until 1933, at the University of Maryland as well. Other than these posts, she had no job in her field until 1935.

Still, despite the hard times, the family was together. Rachel's sister, Marian, was divorced, and

she and her children spent some of these years in the family home. The Carson family, which at one time had stood around the piano at the old farmhouse singing harmony after dinner, could still join in a song now and then.

But on July 6, 1935, everything changed for the Carsons. That day Rachel's father walked out the back door of the house and, on his way across the yard, collapsed. He died of a heart attack there in Maria Carson's arms. From that moment on, Rachel would assume new and much greater family responsibilities. She would have to support her mother, as well as herself.

Rachel Carson in 1932 while she was a graduate student at The Johns Hopkins University.

Chapter/Four

We glimpsed a new way of seeing our world

Rachel Carson needed a job now more than ever. She made an appointment with Elmer Higgins at the Bureau of Fisheries. "I happened in one morning when the chief of the biology division was feeling rather desperate," she recalled years later.

The Bureau of Fisheries was trying to produce radio broadcasts explaining marine life. They had hired a professional radio writer who was not a scientist, and he had quickly run out of things to say. Higgins assigned the job to some of the bureau's staff scientists. But they were scientists, not writers, and did not know how to write lively, interesting stories. By this time the staff was calling the broadcasts the "seven-minute fish tales," though officially they were titled "Romance Under the Waters."

Higgins had no one else to turn to for the broadcast writing.

"I think at that point he was having to write the scripts himself," Carson said. So when Rachel Carson walked into his office to talk about a job, he welcomed her. "He talked to me a few minutes and then said: 'I've never seen a written word of yours, but I'm going to take a sporting chance.' That little job," Carson went on, "which eventually led to a permanent appointment as a biologist, was in its way, a turning point."

Carson returned home from her meeting with Higgins and sat down to write. A week later, she was back in Higgins's office with the finished "fish tales." Higgins liked them and assigned her more. She worked out of her home, coming into the bureau for meetings and to turn in her work. It wasn't a full-time job, and she still worked that summer teaching at Johns Hopkins's summer school, but it was a good beginning. When the bureau decided to turn the broadcasts into a brochure, Higgins assigned that project to Carson also.

The next time the U.S. government civil service examination was given, Rachel took it, hoping to qualify for an opening at the bureau for a junior aquatic biologist. The position would be perfect for her, since it combined her degrees in zoology and biology and her specialty in marine wildlife. She was the only woman taking the test, and she scored well on it. In fact, her score was the highest—higher than any of the men who took it that day.

Carson had a job. Higgins asked to have her in his office, and she became a full-time, permanent U.S. civil service employee. Her salary, starting August 17, 1936, was $2,000 per year. At last, she and her mother, though not rich by any measurement, had at least a little financial security. Rachel had her own desk, her own professional responsibilities, and a schedule that required her to report to work every weekday morning.

Staying inside all day was an adjustment for Carson, who had spent so much of her life outdoors exploring the world around her. Her office was small and had just one window. The window faced an interior courtyard that was surrounded by the high walls of the building. Working there, Carson commented one day to a colleague, was "like working in the bottom of a well."

Her job was to answer questions people sent in to the bureau. Many of the questions could be answered simply by sending the person a brochure. Others involved research and individual answers.

When she started work at the bureau, Rachel and her mother moved to Silver Spring, Maryland, which was closer to Carson's job in Washington, D.C., than the house in Baltimore had been. Maria Carson took care of the cooking—Rachel hated to cook—and Maria also did the cleaning and shopping.

"Mrs. Carson was a great help," recalled Shirley Briggs, Rachel's friend and colleague. "Most professional women of that period and maybe now couldn't have done it if they hadn't had a mother or mother-in-law or family or some sort of support system," Shirley added. "Men have wives. Women [too] need someone to rally 'round."

Rachel's job at the bureau gave her and her mother a steady income, but they still lived on a tight budget. Carson earned extra money by writing for the Sunday magazine section of the *Baltimore Sun*. She wrote articles about local fishing conditions and conservation. Her first was headlined, "It'll be Shad-Time Soon—And Chesapeake Bay Fishermen Hope for Better Luck this Season." She wrote many others, with titles such as, "Numbering the Fish of the Sea" and "Farming Under the Chesapeake."

Money, always a problem, soon became more important than ever. Rachel's sister, Marian, who had been ill for years, died just as Rachel was settling into her new role as chief provider for herself and her mother. Marian was just forty, and her daughters, Marian Virginia Williams and Marjorie Louise Williams, were both still in grammar school. Rachel and her mother discussed what should be done about the children, and Maria encouraged Rachel to take them in. Rachel did. Now her household included four members, and her mother again began to raise two young girls.

Rachel Carson was about thirty years of age, not very old for a person with the responsibilities she now had. She was the working member, the sole provider, for herself, her mother, and her two nieces as well. If she had had hopes of traveling to faraway lands or exploring the vast oceans of the world, she now put them aside. She became a model employee at the Bureau of Fisheries and a generous, good-humored aunt at home.

Carson's fish tales ran on radio broadcasts for a year. Higgins, after reviewing a booklet of tales Carson had created, asked her to write an introduction that would pull all the elements together. Carson set about the task. As she wrote, she said, "somehow the material rather took charge of the situation and turned into something that was, perhaps, unusual as a broadcast for the Commissioner of Fisheries."

She handed her introduction to Higgins for his approval, but, she said, he "handed it back with a twinkle in his eye. 'I don't think it will do,' he said. 'Better try again.' " Carson was unpleasantly surprised because she thought her introduction was well written. Then Higgins added, "send this one to the *Atlantic*." Carson smiled. Higgins did like her work. In fact, he thought it was *too* good. He was talking about sending her work to a well known and highly respected national magazine, the *Atlantic Monthly*.

Carson took her introduction home and hid it in a drawer. She wasn't quite ready to send it to the *Atlantic*. She wrote another introduction for the fish tales booklet, though, doing the work at home, since she now owned the work she had completed at work.

Rachel held onto the introduction until 1937. Then she pulled it out of its hiding place one day, rewrote it somewhat, popped it into an envelope, and mailed it to the magazine.

She had a six-week wait before she received an answer from the *Atlantic Monthly*, but it was an answer well worth the waiting. Her article would appear in the September 1937 issue, the letter said. And Rachel held in her hand a check for $75 in payment.

Carson's article, as published in the *Atlantic Monthly*, evoked a feeling of what it meant to live in the ocean:

To sense this world of waters known to the creatures
of the sea we must shed our human perceptions of
length and breadth and time and place, and enter vi-
cariously into a universe of all-pervading water. For to
the sea's children nothing is so important as the fluid-
ity of their world. It is water that they breathe; water
that brings them food; water through which they see,
by filtered sunshine from which first the red rays, then
the greens, and finally the purples have been strained;
water through which they sense vibrations equivalent
to sound...

From that first article accepted by this national
magazine, "everything else followed," Carson later
said. This was indeed a high point in her life.

Paul Brooks, editor of her later works, commented on the importance of the moment to Carson. "After a lapse of twenty-five years, the incident
was still vivid in her memory," he remembered.
Some events are so important that every little detail
remains clear forever. For Rachel Carson, this was
one of those events.

"Quincy Howe, then editor for Simon and
Schuster, wrote to ask why I didn't do a book,"
Carson recalled. "So did Hendrik Willem van Loon
[a famous author]. My mail had never contained
anything so exciting as his first letter." That letter
arrived in an envelope "adorned with a bright green
seascape from which a blue whale and perhaps a

shark or two looked forth," Carson said.

Rachel Carson traveled to Old Greenwich for a meeting with van Loon and Howe. She spent "a memorable two days with the van Loons," she later wrote, "during which time Mr. and Mrs. Howe came to dinner." They surprised Rachel by urging her to write a book expanding on her *Atlantic* article.

A book! When Rachel had changed majors in college to become a scientist, she thought she was giving up her dream of becoming a writer. She did not consider the brochures and newspaper columns she wrote every day at her job as "writing"; they were simply collections of information. But to write a book about the sea—that would be writing in the fullest sense of the word.

Carson set to work producing an outline and sample chapters for Simon and Schuster, a New York publishing company. These were required before the publisher could sign a contract with her. Rachel worked evenings and weekends, after her full day's work at the bureau. As always, the need for money drove her to accept whatever work was offered, so she continued to write the newspaper stories for the *Baltimore Sun.* She wrote at least seven of them in 1938, with her mother helping as much as she could. Though Maria Carson was almost seventy years old, she typed her daughter's manuscripts in addition to doing all the housekeeping and taking care of Marjorie and Virginia.

Rachel Carson was later to look back on these years as carefree ones, in spite of the pressures of work and her extra writing projects. She had the excitement of creating a book, and still had the time to get away for a few hours of hiking and bird watching. Often her mother would go with her, and sometimes Marjorie would, too.

"A foray along the shore or through the spruce woods [with Carson] was always high adventure," wrote Shirley Briggs, who joined the U.S. Fish and Wildlife Service in 1945 and became great friends with Carson. "We who were included in her own expeditions learned a great deal about many aspects of our world, but most of all a way of seeing, alert for every impression, with keen delight in all manner of small creatures as well as the vast horizons and far reaches."

Rachel Carson saw the world on an ecological level. All things were connected, all things related. It was not enough to look at a bird and see how fine its feathers glistened in the sunshine. To truly appreciate the bird, one had to know what that bird ate, where it nested, how it mated, how it raised its young, where it spent its winters and summers, and even how it affected the tree in which it lived. What one creature did affected every other creature and living thing around it.

Carson included some of these thoughts in the book she was writing. She worked hard on the book, but she "kept it very much to herself," said a colleague at the Woods Hole fisheries laboratory. The colleague added that everyone "was getting more and more curious but knew nothing more until the book was published." Then, upon seeing it, Rachel's friends "were very surprised and tremendously excited."

Rachel herself always maintained a special love for her first book. She explained her feelings to a friend: "I need to lose myself completely in what I am writing....I came nearest to achieving that complete losing of myself in writing the *Sea-Wind*."

The title of her book was to be *Under the Sea-Wind*. In the book's original foreword, Rachel explained what she was trying to create. It "was written to make the sea and its life as vivid a reality for those who may read the book as it has become for me during the past decade," she wrote. To sense the sea, feel it, breathe it, watch the shore birds and the "running of old eels and young shad to the sea, is to have knowledge of things that are as nearly eternal as any earthly life can be. These things were before ever man stood on the shore of the ocean and looked out upon it with wonder; they continue year in, year out, through the centuries and the ages, while man's kingdoms rise and fall."

Carson's deadline for the book was the fall of 1940. She worked to meet the deadline, at a desk set up in a large, second-story bedroom of her house. Often she worked late at night, after the noises of the family had ceased for the night. "My only companions during those otherwise solitary sessions were two precious Persian cats, Buzzie and Kito," she said. The two cats "took turns" lying on Carson's manuscripts. "Buzzie in particular used to sleep on my writing table, on the litter of notes and manuscript sheets." At odd moments, while she searched her mind for a phrase or word to express the ocean for *Sea-Wind*, she sketched little pictures of her cat. Then she turned back to her typewriter.

While Buzzie and Kito were keeping Carson company through the long nights, the world around them was growing stormy once again. Adolph Hitler's Nazi concentration camps were already in full operation, and his troops were marching across Europe. For the second time in Carson's life, the world was at war.

When Rachel Carson submitted her finished

Rachel Carson works on a manuscript at home.

manuscript in the fall of 1940, the United States had not declared war but was sending supplies to Great Britain to help in the battle against Hitler. *Under the Sea-Wind* was published a year later, on November 1, 1941. Reviews were positive. "I have thoroughly enjoyed every word of the volume," wrote Dr. William Beebe, a well-known author and scientist who reviewed the book for the *Saturday Review* magazine.

But the book's timing was bad. When the Japanese attacked the U.S. navy base at Pearl Harbor on December 7, 1941, the conflict tore the nation's attention away from the beauties of the ocean. The country was at war.

"The world received [*Under the Sea-Wind*] with superb indifference," Carson later said. In the first year the book sold 1,348 copies, and from the entire first printing Carson made less than $1,000. But if sales were disappointing, the enthusiastic response of the scientific community was heartwarming. Carson's book was made a Scientific Book Club selection in October 1942, and Dr. William Beebe included two chapters from it in his anthology, *The Book of Naturalists*. Though it wasn't a success with the American public, it was read and appreciated by knowledgable readers in the field.

Chapter/Five

In the mood to make a change

Even for Rachel Carson, *Under the Sea-Wind* had but a brief life. The world around her demanded all her attention. Wartime Washington, D.C., was a hectic place. Those departments that contributed directly to the war effort were expanded. Others were reorganized to make room for the swelling populations of military and technical experts that now occupied the city. Carson was promoted to assistant aquatic biologist in 1942, and her department was slated for a move to temporary quarters in Chicago, Illinois. Like many Americans of the time, Carson wanted to do as much as possible to help the war effort. "In many ways, I'd rather get into some sort of work that had more immediate value in relation to the war," she said. Still, she stayed with her department and in 1942 moved to Chicago.

Carson went to work on a new project for the Bureau of Fisheries, which had been renamed the Fish and Wildlife Service. She began writing a series of pamphlets describing the nutritional values of fish and shellfish. During the war, meat was needed for the soldiers overseas, so back home there were shortages. The U.S. government wanted to encourage Americans to eat fish in place of meat.

Rachel Carson confessed that she never really cared for fish as food, but the information she included in the booklets helped many Americans learn to cook and appreciate fish for dinner. Her tips and recipes were picked up and repeated by countless radio announcers, magazines, and newspapers.

Back in Washington, D.C., once more in 1943, Carson was promoted to associate aquatic biologist. Then in 1945, the year the war ended, she was promoted to aquatic biologist. Meanwhile, she had found time to write a few magazine articles, including an article about bats and their radar for *Reader's Digest.*

Rachel was restless with her job at the Fish and Wildlife Service. "I'm definitely in the mood to make a change of some sort, preferably to something that will give me more time for my own writing," she wrote to a friend. Rachel was clearly ready to do more than work for the government. What could she do next, she asked herself, without risking her financial security?

In spite of her desire for a change, Carson realized, too, that she enjoyed some aspects of her job. She had made some close friends at work. Her office had improved with her promotions, and she and her co-workers found time at lunch and breaks to let off steam. In-office jokes and humor prevailed as the editorial staff made fun of the bureaucracy that enmeshed them. Frustrations and needless red tape became the subject of their jokes. Together, they formed a close-knit, friendly office group.

Off hours, too, Carson was included in a round of parties and weekend activities. "Looking back at the records, I was astonished at the number of parties we had," said Shirley Briggs. "And Rachel was always there if possible....Rachel appreciated so many kinds of people, and was always glad to meet new ones and enter into whatever conversation or merriment was going on at these affairs."

Rachel was a "thoroughly delightful person," Briggs recalled. And she "had very nice, respectable gentlemen friends who took her out." Rachel Carson never married any of them, though. Once she told a reporter she had simply been too busy. "She was very involved with her family," said Briggs. In addition, she had responsibilities at work and also an ambition to write books. "When she said she just never had time to get married," Briggs added, "that's probably exactly right."

Shirley Briggs and Rachel Carson became great friends because they shared an interest in the outdoors. One of the first field trips Carson and Briggs took together for the Fish and Wildlife Service was in fall 1945, when they traveled to the Pennsylvania Hawk Mountain Sanctuary. On their first day there, they climbed out of bed before dawn, filled thermoses with coffee for the chilly day to come on the mountain, and traveled to a high spot to catch a glimpse of the hawks that populated the mountain. It was a beautiful sight.

"[The hawks] came by like brown leaves drifting on the wind," Carson noted. "...Second by second the outlines sharpen. Soon the unmistakable silhouette of a hawk is etched on the gray...Sometimes he banks steeply and his outlines melt into the sky...

"I settle back against the rock behind me, seeking shelter from the wind, trying vainly to draw some physical comfort from the hard angularity [sharp edges] of stone. The cold is bitter....But

High on Hawk Mountain, Carson scans the sky for the hawks soaring over this wildlife sanctuary.

cold, windy weather is hawk weather, and so I am glad, although I shiver and my nose reddens..."

These rugged expeditions were a welcome contrast to the quiet yet intense days Carson spent in the office editing Fish and Wildlife Service publications. The service's budget could never pay for as many field trips as Carson would have liked, but once in a while she would go on a truly great one. The Hawk Mountain Sanctuary trip was one such memorable trip. So was the one that Rachel Carson made with Shirley Briggs to the Florida Everglades.

On that trip. Carson and Briggs explored the Everglades in a "glades buggy." According to Carson, this contraption "was built something like a tractor, with six pairs of very large wheels. Its engine was completely naked and exposed, and during the trip blasted its heat on the three of us [Carson, Briggs, and the driver] perched on the buggy's single seat."

It was the first time the driver had ever taken females out into the huge swamp on his buggy. He hesitated and tried to get rid of Carson by warning her it would be an uncomfortable trip, but Carson's desire to go prevailed. Rachel was usually described as ladylike and genteel. Yet when she decided she was going to do something, she became determined. That determination had helped her stand up to the president and the teachers at the Pennsylvania College for Women who tried to persuade her not to become a scientist. On this day in Florida, it got her out onto the Everglades.

The Everglades were fascinating, but the ocean was Rachel Carson's first love. Outside of work, she tried to spend as much time by the sea as possible. During the summer of 1946, she and her mother rented a seaside cabin on the Sheepscot River near Boothbay, Maine. "Our little place is on the very edge of the water—if you jumped out of the windows on one side you would fall in," Carson wrote to Shirley Briggs. It was a wonderful cabin, but even more wonderful was the world around it—the hillsides with spruce and birch trees, the nearby ocean, the seagulls, herons, and ospreys, and the sound of bell buoys. "And—when the wind is right, the very distant sound of surf," wrote Carson.

Rachel had found her way to her own form of paradise, the seashore. She explored the area's tide pools, and when exhausted with that, lay on the beach and watched the birds overhead. "On warm sunny days the gulls go so high they look about the size of stars," she wrote. "Sometimes a dark star comes into sight, and that is an osprey.

"From all this you will know that the only reason I will ever come back is that I don't have brains enough to figure out a way to stay here the rest of my life," Carson concluded. "At least I know now that my greatest ambition is to be able to buy a place here and then manage to spend a great deal of time in it—summers at least!"

Chapter/Six

The surface of the water... from underneath

"No, my life isn't at all well ordered and I don't know where I am going! I know that if I could choose what seems to me the ideal existence, it would be just to live by writing. But I have done far too little to dare risk it. And all the while my job with the service grows and demands more and more of me...," Carson wrote to a friend.

Her position, indeed, had grown more responsible. In 1946 she was promoted to information specialist. In 1949, she was appointed editor-in-chief. Rachel had come a long way from her first days in a small cubbyhole of an office. Now her office was spacious and well lighted, her desk a large table. She sat facing into the room, with tall windows behind her. Bookshelves lined the two long

walls of her office, and on her wall hung a photograph of a blue crab. Carson directed the opera-
tions of the Fish and Wildlife Service's publishing
program. She worked with authors and supervised
six staff members who handled the details of illustrating, laying out, designing, and editing the
publications.

Carson worked with people and groups outside her official duties, too. She served as director
of her local Audubon Naturalist Society's board.
And, according to the late Howard Zahniser of the
Wilderness Society, she also wrote many congres-
sional speeches on subjects in her field for government officials.

At the Fish and Wildlife Service, she was producing a series of twelve booklets, "Conservation in
Action," which included information about some of
the country's 300 national wildlife refuges. Carson
had strong feelings about this subject. Many times in
the past she had looked out over a forest or a coast-
line and worried about its future. Her work on the
service's booklets gave her an opportunity to express
that philosophy. "All the people of a country have a
direct interest in conservation," she wrote.

> For some, as for the commercial fishermen and trap-
> pers, the interest is financial. For others, successful
> conservation means preserving a favorite recreation—

> hunting, fishing, the study and observation of wildlife, or nature photography....But for all the people, the preservation of wildlife and wildlife habitat means also the preservation of the basic resources of the earth, which men, as well as animals, must have in order to live. Wildlife, water, forests, grasslands—all are parts of man's essential environment...

Rachel Carson was forty-two years old in 1949. She had a responsible job, the respect of her colleagues, and a life rich with a love of nature. She also had the time to do some of the things she loved—birdwatching, nature exploring, and hiking. Still, she yearned to break away and live by her writing. Once again, she began to work on a book.

By the time Carson signed a contract with the Oxford University Press in 1949, she was already hard at work on the new book. Bob Hines, her illustrator at the Fish and Wildlife Service, became a vital link for her to local libraries. He would bring her stacks of books, pile them in the back seat of her car in the afternoon before she drove home, and then exchange them for a new stack a few days later. Although many of the books were highly technical, scientific works, Carson seemed able to read and glean information from them all in surprisingly short time spans. Even Carson herself admitted that her book required "an immense amount of research material." Before it was finished, she estimated that she consulted "more than a thousand separate printed sources." She also corresponded with experts in oceanography.

Rachel wrote at night and on weekends, working as hard and as long as she could—she had to get enough sleep to be alert for her Fish and Wildlife Service job, too. In the room with her were her faithful friends, her cats. She later said that "more than once I asked myself why I had ever undertaken such an unending task."

Rachel would eventually call her new book *The Sea Around Us*. By her own estimate, it took her about two years to write from the time she outlined it to the day she delivered the completed manuscript to Oxford University Press. But, she added, "in a sense, I have been collecting material for this ocean book all my life—ever since childhood I've been fascinated by the sea and my mind has stored up everything I have ever learned about it as well as my own thoughts, impressions, and emotions."

Carson was a slow, painstaking writer. She rewrote every chapter many times. Often at the end of a writing "day" she would have completed only 500 words (two typewritten pages); other times as many as 1,500 words. And often, when she sat staring at the typewriter and couldn't make the words come at all, she pulled out paper and pencil. The familiar feel of a pencil between her fingers would help her concentrate, and she would see the words begin to follow one another across the pages. "My best hours for writing are late at night," Carson said, "and whenever I could get an uninterrupted period of time for working on "The Sea" I would work most of each night and sleep in the mornings."

Night by night, *The Sea Around Us* slowly took shape. And yet, Carson realized that to write the book well, she would need to do more than just library and correspondence research. Dr. William Beebe, who had praised *Under the Sea-Wind*, advised her that to write a book about underwater life she needed to go underwater and experience the ocean firsthand. Beebe had gone deep-sea diving many times; in fact, he was something of an underseas celebrity. Photos of him in a bathysphere (a diving compartment) or a diving suit were familiar sights. After visiting him in New York in April 1949, Rachel Carson agreed with him.

"I don't dare finish this book without getting under water," she wrote to Marie Rodell, her literary agent. Though Carson had studied the ocean all her life, she was not a great swimmer. What's more, ocean diving in 1949 was not as advanced as it is today. Carson wore a bulky diving helmet and breathed air pumped down to her through a connecting tube. She also wore weights on her feet to pull her down through the water. Carson went down just fifteen feet, but for an author with her imagination, that was enough. "There I learned what the surface of the water looks like from underneath," she later wrote, "and how exquisitely delicate and varied are the colors displayed by the animals of the reef, and I got the feeling of the misty green vistas of a strange, nonhuman world."

Also that summer, Rachel Carson spent ten days on the Fish and Wildlife Service's research vessel, the *Albatross III*, taking a census of the fish population. No woman had ever been a part of the fifty-man *Albatross* team before. Marie Rodell went with her on the expedition because the Fish and Wildlife Service thought it would be more proper for two women to go on the voyage than just one. The *Albatross* fished night and day, collecting information along with the fish the crew pulled in with their nets.

The men were not pleased to have these two women aboard, and warned them that life on the *Albatross* could be a very rugged, uncomfortable experience. The food was bad, and the ocean's rolling waves made most "landlubbers" seasick. The ship's machinery was heavy, and fingers and toes could

With a bulky diving helmet beside her, Rachel Carson goes on a diving expedition during her research for The Sea Around Us.

easily get crushed under it. Worst of all was the noise! Day and night, chains dragged across the deck as the men worked. Many of the stories they told, Carson said, turned out to be true—especially about the noisiness of the fishing.

She and Marie Rodell were sound asleep when the first night's fishing began. "We heard a crash," Carson said. "...Surely we had been rammed by another vessel. Then a series of the most appalling bangs, clunks, and rumbles began directly over our heads, a rhythmic thundering of machinery that would put any boiler factory to shame. Finally it dawned on us that this was fishing! It also dawned on us that this was what we had to endure for the next ten nights...."

"At breakfast the next morning there were grins on the faces of the men. 'Hear anything last night?' they asked. Both of us wore our most demure expressions. 'Well,' said Marie, 'once we thought we heard a mouse, but we were too sleepy to bother.' They never asked us again. And after a night or two we really did sleep through the uproar like old salts."

It had been an eventful summer for Rachel Carson. She had gone diving, had traveled the high seas on a research voyage, and had written and gathered material for her book. Though she hoped to finish it soon, completing the remaining work proved to be a difficult task.

One of her nieces became ill and needed Rachel's attention. Then Rachel and her family moved to a different house in Silver Spring. Through it all, her job at the Fish and Wildlife Service continued to be demanding. As week followed week and those grew into months, Carson worked harder than ever; still the goal was always just another few months away. In mid-February she wrote to Marie Rodell. "None of the present or future is very favorable for the last desperate push, but I am grimly determined to finish somehow."

In May, she was still hard at work on the book. "Not a single morning bird walk and spring almost gone!" she wrote. "I am really upset about it, but don't seem to have the energy to tuck that in, too." Birdwatching was one of Rachel Carson's keenest enjoyments. "I consider few pleasures equal to early morning 'birding' during the spring migration season," she once admitted.

Maria Carson helped her daughter out as much as she could. In fact, she typed the entire manuscript for the book—typing up the only perfect manuscript the Oxford University Press had ever received, according to Shirley Briggs. Finally, in July 1950, Rachel finished her writing. Maria Carson finished typing, and the manuscript was ready for the publisher.

The Sea Around Us covered an enormous number and variety of subjects. In it, Carson explained what scientists knew up to that time about the creation of the oceans, as well as the sea life that exists in the surface waters and in the ocean depths. She wrote about currents, tides, and wind. She described the effect the oceans have on Earth's great masses of land, and the effects humans can have on the oceans. Carson wrote the book so that anyone who read it could see the ocean's beauty as she saw it, and could experience its mystery, and its suspense. She wrote about the vast reaches of the ocean, and also about the incredible numbers of tiny, microscopic creatures that live in its life-sustaining waters. Here is the passage that begins a chapter about islands:

> Millions of years ago, a volcano built a mountain on the floor of the Atlantic. In eruption after eruption, it pushed up a great pile of volcanic rock, until it had accumulated a mass a hundred miles across at its base, reaching upward toward the surface of the sea. Finally its cone emerged as an island with an area of about 200 square miles. Thousands of years passed, and thousands of thousands. Eventually the waves of the Atlantic cut down the cone and reduced it to a shoal— all of it, that is, but a small fragment which remained above water. This fragment we know as Bermuda.

Carson ends a chapter about tides with these thoughts:

> What I find most unforgettable about Convoluta [*Convoluta roscoffensis*, a small, flat, green worm] is this: sometimes it happens that a marine biologist, wishing to study some related problem, will transfer a whole colony of the worms into the laboratory, there to establish them in an aquarium, where there are no tides. But twice each day Convoluta rises out of the sand on the bottom of the aquarium, into the light of the sun. And twice each day it sinks again into the sand. Without a brain, or what we would call a memory, or even any very clear perception, Convoluta continues to live out its life in this alien place, remembering, in every fiber of its small green body, the tidal rhythm of the distant sea.

Carson's agent, Marie Rodell, sent sample chapters to magazines to see if any of them would be interested in publishing an excerpt (a short section) from the book. The manuscript was rejected by a number of well-known magazines before Rodell sold a chapter to the *Yale Review*. When that chapter was published, it won the American Association for the Advancement of Science George Westinghouse Science Writing Award for the "finest example of science writing in any American magazine in 1950." Soon Rodell also sold rights to print excerpts to *Science Digest*, and then to the *New Yorker*.

When a three-part series of condensed chapters from *The Sea Around Us* appeared in the *New Yorker*, Rachel Carson's life changed forever. The magazine paid her about as much for the excerpts of her book as she made in a year at her job with the Fish and Wildlife Service. Suddenly it seemed that the entire country wanted to know more about the amazing scientist who had written this stunning article.

The book itself was published July 2, 1951. The *New York Times Book Review*, which had received an advance copy, featured a story about it in its July 1, 1951, issue. The science editor, Jonathan Norton Leonard, praised the book as a wonderful blend of poetry and science. "Every person who reads it will look on the sea with new pleasure. He will know that it is full of lights and sounds and movements, of sunken lands and mountains, of the debris of meteors, of plains strewn with ancient sharks' teeth and the ear-bones of whales."

Leonard expressed, too, a curiosity that Carson had not expected. He wanted to know what this wonderful scientist looked like. "It's a pity that the book's publishers did not print on its jacket a photograph," he wrote.

As the book's fame grew and more and more people read it, this same curiosity cropped up again and again. Some people assumed the author was a man. Some pictured her as gray-haired and terribly dignified, while others thought she must be a large, forbidding figure. Shirley Briggs presented Rachel Carson with a painting of what her readers thought she looked like—a large, lean, robust woman standing on a windswept shore, an octopus in one hand, and a spear in the other.

Chapter/Seven

A hectic but wonderful existence

Rachel Carson, suddenly a famous author, was caught up in a frenzy of events. *Reader's Digest* offered her $10,000 for the right to publish a condensed form of *The Sea Around Us*. The book was chosen as an alternate selection by the Book-of-the-Month Club. Everyone, it seemed, was talking about Rachel Carson and her poetic book about the ocean.

Carson was invited to be a guest speaker at a number of lunches, banquets, and receptions. She was presented with honorary doctorates from her own college, from Oberlin College, and from the Drexel Institute for Technology. She autographed books in November, presenting the 100,000th copy of her book to a Cleveland department store cus-

Sitting on a dock at Woods Hole, Massachusetts, Carson helps create publicity for her latest book, The Sea Around Us.

tomer. Everyone wanted to meet this suddenly famous scientist, the author of a book that the *New York Times* Christmas poll voted "the outstanding book of the year." Her book soon appeared on the *New York Times* best-seller list, a position it would hold for eighty-six weeks. Carson also won the John Burroughs Medal (an award for natural history writing), and the National Book Award for the best nonfiction book of the year.

"Many people have commented with surprise on the fact that a work of science should have a large popular sale," Carson said in her speech accepting the National Book Award. "But this notion, that 'science' is something that belongs in a separate compartment of its own, apart from everyday life, is one that I should like to challenge. We live in a scientific age...Science is part of the reality of living: it is the what, the how, and the why of everything in our experience..."

All the speeches and appearances were exciting experiences, but they were exhausting, too. Carson, a private person by nature, was surprised at the unending attention she received. At one point, she reported, a fan found out what motel she was staying at, knocked on the door, and when Carson's mother answered it, barged past her and pushed two books in front of Carson. She wanted them autographed. Carson, still in bed, was courteous to the fan, but she was also quite annoyed at the intrusion.

In April 1952, her publisher re-released her first book, *Under the Sea-Wind*. Now that the author was famous, and there was no world war to distract the readers of the country, *Under the Sea-Wind* sold rapidly. Like *The Sea Around Us*, it was chosen as an alternate Book-of-the-Month Club selection. Then Carson had two books on the best-seller list.

All the attention that was focused on this new author did not go unnoticed by the movie studios in

Hollywood. RKO bought the rights to make a film of *The Sea Around Us*. Carson was delighted by the idea, until she saw the final result. She found many errors in the film, several of which she and her agent, Marie Rodell, corrected before the film was released. She was never pleased with the film, though it won an Oscar for the best full-length documentary of 1953.

Nevertheless, with two best sellers and an Oscar-winning film to her credit, Carson was truly a celebrity. It was "a hectic, but wonderful existence," said her colleague, illustrator Bob Hines. Carson had taken a year's leave of absence from her job in June 1951, after she had begun to receive checks from magazines for excerpts and from her publisher for book royalties. She realized that at last she really could "live by writing." Rachel Carson was an author, and a richly famous one at that. In June 1952, she officially resigned from her position as editor-in-chief at the U.S. Fish and Wildlife Service.

Already, she had begun to work on her next book. She spent most of the summer of 1952 at the Woods Hole laboratory, once again searching through the library's shelves for detailed information about the sea life that would fill her new book. It began, Carson later recalled, "as a subconscious thought somewhere deep in my mind that I would one day do a different sort of book about the shore." She saw the book as more than just a guide. She would call it *The Edge of the Sea*, and in it, she said, she wanted "to take the seashore out of the category of scenery and make it come alive." Carson decided on an ecological approach; she would show how the animals lived and depended on each other and the ocean's tides. She would talk about where they lived, what they ate, and which animals were their enemies and their friends.

Rachel Carson soon fulfilled another dream, too. She bought an acre and a half of land at West Southport, Maine, on the west shore of Boothbay Harbor, and she built a one-story house on it. Behind her was a seaside forest of tall trees, in front was a rugged cliff, and beyond that the ocean. Stairs led down to the beach. From the house, every window looked out at a view of the sea.

In contrast to the hectic days she spent promoting *The Sea Around Us*, days here at Boothbay Harbor could be carefree and relaxing. Often, Rachel and her mother would carry a paper bag of food down the stairs to the beach to feed the sea gulls that flew above the harbor in search of food. Rachel would walk out onto the open beach and slowly, quietly, swing the paper bag in long, high circles. Soon the gulls would see the enticing movements

Rachel Carson explores a tidepool near her summer home in West Southport, Maine.

of the bag, and would fly toward her. Some would catch bread crusts thrown into the air; others would take the food directly from Rachel's hand.

Rachel Carson spent as much time as she could beside the ocean. She would travel to different areas along the nearby coast, reaching them at low tide. Often her mother would accompany her in the car. While Rachel was below at the water's edge collecting specimens, Maria Carson, too fragile to stay outside with Rachel, would stay in the car to write letters. Sometimes, on meeting others who had come to gaze out at the ocean from the road above, she would point down at the slight figure bending

over the tidepools. That was her daughter, the famous Rachel Carson, she would tell the visitors.

Marjorie and Virginia, Rachel's nieces, had
grown up and lived in other places by this time.
Rachel and her mother usually saw them only on
holidays when the young women might come to
join them at the seashore or stop in at the house in
Silver Springs. Once again Rachel's immediate family was a small one—just her, her mother, and, as
always, at least one cat.

Whether at work on her book about ocean
coastal zones, or at play, Carson enjoyed exploring
tidepools. "I can't think of any more exciting place
to be than down in the low-tide world, when the
ebb tide falls very early in the morning, and the
world is full of salt smell, and the sound of water,
and the softness of fog," she once said.

Bob Hines, who often accompanied Rachel
when he was illustrating *The Edge of the Sea*, recalled
that often she would become fascinated by her explorations and would lose track of time. The cold
tidepools of the Maine coastal waters circling her
ankles, her hands happily dimpled from long ex-
posure to the wet salt water, she would bend for
hours over the shore's tiny life forms, examining
them through a magnifying glass. More than once
her body became so numb and stiff from the cold

During her research for The Edge of the Sea, *Carson and Bob Hines examine the life in a tidepool.*

seawater that Bob Hines had to carry her ashore.

Carson and Hines spent countless hours at America's East Coast beaches examining life in the tidepools, and often collected specimens to take back to the laboratory so Hines could draw them. "*Amphithoe rubricata, Littorina obtusata,* and *Diadema antillarum*" were some of the names scientists called the creatures of the tidepools. "Wee beasts," Hines called them all, with both affection for them, and despair of memorizing their difficult names. Carson would bring a bucket and wear a belt that held bottles and flasks for carrying home the specimens she and Hines collected. She would later return the creatures to their tidepools, often feeling her way back with a flashlight at night to catch the evening low tide.

Rachel enjoyed many entertaining evenings, after a day at the tidepools, bending over her microscope to examine the creatures. She would sit enraptured for hours as she watched them live out their tiny lives—eating, chasing prey, raising young.

She shared some of her tidepool discoveries with Dorothy and Stanley Freeman, two of her summertime neighbors at the shore. Both were specialists in agriculture—Dorothy had worked for the U.S. Department of Agriculture, Stanley for a feed company. Since the Freemans shared a great

Rachel Carson observes specimens from tidepools through a microscope. She would later return the "wee beasts" to their tidepools.

appreciation of nature with Rachel Carson, the three soon became close friends. They went on picnics, went sailing in Stanley's boat, and often sat on the porch watching the sun set and applauding when the moon rose.

Dorothy brought Rachel to one of her favorite tidepools on the shore. Carson described it in *The Edge of the Sea*. She called it a "fairy pool" because it was so delicate and so seldom seen. "The floor of the cave was only a few inches below the roof, and a mirror had been created in which all that grew on the ceiling was reflected in the still water below," she wrote. Green sponges and "gray patches of sea squirts" dwelled in this tiny oceanside cave. As she watched, Carson saw a tiny "elfin starfish" lower itself on a tiny thread from the ceiling to touch its reflection in the water below. Stanley, an amateur photographer, crawled out on the slim ledge to take pictures of the cave for Carson.

Carson dedicated her book to Dorothy and Stanley Freeman. She described them as two friends "who have gone down with me into the low-tide world and have felt its beauty and its mystery."

The few years since *The Sea Around Us* was published had been busy, happy years in Carson's life. Her financial worries were over; she was at work on *The Edge of the Sea*, a project she loved;

she had two wonderful friends to spend her summer holiday with; and her mother, though handicapped with arthritis, was with her still.

The Edge of the Sea, like *The Sea Around Us*, was published in the *New Yorker* before it was released as a book. Once more, Rachel Carson had an award-winning book in bookstores across the nation.

"The edge of the sea is a strange and beautiful place," her book began. And then it described the unusual creatures that live on the shoreline—creatures that live underwater when the tide is in, and above water when the tide is out. Starfish, anemones, periwinkles, limpets, sponges, corals, and many other animals and plants—all have their place at the edge of the sea.

Carson hoped that after reading the book, people visiting the seashore would remember the animals that lived there and would be careful not to harm them. Even the tough, craggy old barnacles that grow on rocks and boat bottoms, she reminded us, are really tiny animals. Inside those hard little volcano-like shells live tiny creatures busily reaching out with feathery "limbs" to catch food floating by in the water. They form one link in the abundant and fragile chain of life where the sea meets the shore.

Chapter/Eight

The wild seacoast is vanishing

It was 1955. Dwight D. Eisenhower was president of the United States. Ed Sullivan hosted one of the most popular television shows of the era, and the next year Elvis Presley would sing "Love Me Tender" on the Sullivan Show. Rock 'n roll music played on many of the radio stations. The world was quite a different place than the quiet one Rachel had been born into in 1907. She was now a woman of forty-eight, and a great-aunt as well. Her niece, Marjorie, had a son, Roger, and Rachel found new joys in introducing this new member of the family to the world around him.

While she continued to work on her writing projects, Rachel took time out now to enjoy her moments with Roger and to care for her mother

This photograph of Carson was taken about the time The Edge of the Sea *was published.*

and Marjorie. Rachel's mother's arthritis was quite advanced by this time, and she needed daily care. Marjorie suffered from the disease, too.

In the midst of the sickness, Rachel shared some cherished moments with Marjorie. In a letter to Dorothy and Stanley Freeman, she recounted a night's adventure she and Marjorie had at the beach. The sand was bright with tiny greenish specks of light. Rachel and Marjorie scooped up the sand with their hands, trying to capture the bright little sparks. As they were playing with the sparkles and watching the remarkable lights, Rachel saw one of them rise off the beach. "Look," she said to Marjorie, "one of them has taken to the air!" As Rachel explained in her letter, this flying sparkle turned out to be a firefly blinking its lamp. "He 'thought' the flashes in the water were other fireflies, signaling to him in the age-old manner of fireflies!" Rachel wrote. "Sure enough, he was soon in trouble and we saw his light flashing urgently as he was rolled around in the wet sand....You can guess the rest: I waded in and rescued him...and put him in Roger's bucket to dry."

Rachel and Marjorie brought their firefly up to the house so when it was able to fly again, it would be far away from the sparkles on the beach. That experience had been one of those "hard-to-describe feelings," Rachel wrote. It had been a happy moment shared with Marjorie, an adventurous one watching the mysteries of the night, and a fascinating one observing nature's workings.

Even though there were bright moments during these months, Rachel's life was dominated by the illness of her loved ones. In the fall of 1956, Maria Carson became ill with pneumonia, and wasn't well until Christmas. Rachel had the flu in January, and Roger had the flu the next month. He came to stay with Rachel because Marjorie, who had severe diabetes as well as arthritis, caught pneumonia and had to go to the hospital.

Marjorie died two weeks later. Rachel wrote to her friend and editor, Paul Brooks, about the tragedy. "Marjorie and I were very close all her life, and of course I miss her dreadfully," she wrote. "Among the many changes this has brought is the fact that I shall now adopt Roger as my own; he had lost his father before he could remember him, and in our small family I am the logical one to care for him and, I'm sure, the one who is really closest to him. He does not fully realize the finality of his loss..."

Rachel had seen her father die years before, and then her sister, and now her niece. She would be Roger's stepmother. In addition to her writing, she would be caring for a young, growing boy.

The next summer Rachel wrote an article for *Holiday* magazine about the seashore. In the article Carson described the animals of the coast, and she wrote about her favorite spots on the shores. But, she added, "Unhappily, some of the places of which I have written no longer remain wild and unspoiled. Instead, they have been...cluttered with amusement [stands], refreshment stands, fishing shacks—all the untidy litter of what passes under the name of civilization...On all coasts it is the same. The wild seacoast is vanishing."

She urged people to turn the coastlines into parks and sanctuaries. "For there remains, in this space-age universe, the possibility that man's way is not always the best," she concluded.

Rachel Carson worried about the overdevelopment of the coastal lands and about the pollution that humans were creating. More than ten years before, she had tried to interest *Reader's Digest* in an article about the dangers of DDT (dichloro-diphenyl-trichloroethane), a dangerous pesticide, but the magazine had rejected her proposal.

Carson and other scientists were growing more and more concerned about pesticides and toxic wastes that were polluting the air, land, and water. These scientists were beginning to speak out, but their comments were scattered, and most Americans remained unconcerned.

Rachel Carson was aware of the dangers of pesticides and spoke out in favor of controlling their use when asked. She may have continued to do nothing more than this if she had not received an alarming letter in late 1957. It was from Olga Owens Huckins, a friend who had created a private bird sanctuary in Massachusetts.

The letter described a mosquito-control project in Huckins's neighborhood. A plane had flown over the houses and lawns, spraying them with DDT to kill mosquitoes. The DDT spray struck the songbirds that were nesting in Huckins's yard. What had been a sanctuary for the songbirds and robins became their gas chamber. The birds all died. The spray also killed grasshoppers, bumblebees, and other insects. It killed the mosquitoes, too, but the mosquitoes returned to the neighborhood much faster than any of the other creatures.

Olga Huckins's letter caused Rachel Carson to begin the research that would become an all-consuming cause and a demanding test of her scientific skills and writing talents. This personal crusade would make her known as the founder of today's ecology movement.

Chapter/Nine

You are the lady who started all this

At first Rachel Carson thought she would help the cause of ecology by writing a magazine article warning people of the dangers of DDT. She would tell them about the birds that were dying and about the insects that were growing stronger and were not killed when sprayed with pesticides. But soon she realized that there was too much information for a single article. The subject was so large and complex that she would have to write a book to cover it completely.

"The more I learned about the use of pesticides, the more appalled I became," said Carson. She signed a contract with Houghton Mifflin in May 1958, planning to complete her book within the year. However, her research through letters, interviews with experts, and textbook studies showed her the problem was greater than she had imagined. Carson talked to experts and gathered information from scientists in Europe as well as in America. Every piece of information had to be double-checked, and then checked again. She knew that once her book was in the stores, leaders of the pesticide industry would be ready to criticize her for any mistake they could find.

The pesticide industry had grown into a powerful force in the United States. During World War II, DDT was used as a dust to kill lice on the troops fighting in Europe, and was sprayed over jungle areas to kill malaria-bearing mosquitoes. This powerful pesticide was sprayed on crops to kill insects that would at times have ruined a year's work for a farmer. And in the suburbs, it was dropped in a dense, thick-smelling cloud to kill the mosquitoes that buzzed out on a hot summer's night and bit the arms and legs of children playing on well-tended lawns.

Pesticides were the miracle chemicals. They could save a farmer's crops, kill disease-bearing fleas, ticks, and lice, and scrape the world clean of unwanted pests. Carson found that in one year, more than 600 million pounds of pesticides were produced in the United States.

Carson wanted her book to explain that all life is interlocking, that one species depends on the health of another for its own health. If all the food grown in America was heavily sprayed with pesticides, what effect would that have on people who eat the food? she asked. Carson did not believe that pesticides should never be used, but she did think they should be used responsibly and wisely. It is important, she said, to use pesticides and humankind's scientific advances not just with skill, but also with thoughtfulness.

As she worked on her book, Rachel also faced the toughest times of her own life. In December 1958, about the time that Rachel had first hoped to have her book done, her mother died. Maria Carson was almost ninety years old, Rachel was fifty-one, and in almost all of those fifty-one years, except when she was in college, she had lived with her mother. Upon her mother's death, Rachel Carson, for virtually the first time in her life, was alone.

Two months passed before Rachel Carson was able to work on her book again. When she did, she was aided by thoughts of how important the project had been to her mother. "Knowing how she felt about that will help me to return to it soon, and to carry it to completion," she wrote to a friend.

Carson's work pace had always been slow and

deliberate, but now it became even slower. She had to cope with extremely complex, difficult material, and the job grew even more difficult when she and Roger were sick. Roger was home for the summer, unable to go to camp because of a respiratory infection, and Rachel had sinus trouble.

Carson hired an assistant, Jeanne Davis, to help her, hoping that this would make the work go faster. She also brought in research assistants. Her pace, though slow, was unwavering. She seldom took time off, even for the hikes and bird-watching she enjoyed so much. Once in a while, though, she would take a short break to watch the birds outside her window or to walk just outside her door to see them. Then she would quickly get back to work, back to the piles and piles of facts about pesticides and chemicals with long names such as methoxychlor and dinitrophenol, as well as dichloro-diphenyl-trichloroethane.

Throughout the rest of the time Carson worked on the book, she suffered from what she later called "a catalog of illnesses." At different times she had arthritis, sinus trouble, iritis, viral infections, and an ulcer. But the real blow came in the spring of 1960 when she went for a physical. Rachel was told she had a breast tumor that could be cancerous and had to be removed.

She had surgery to remove it. Her doctor told her after the surgery that the tumor had been benign (not cancerous) and that she was healthy again. But he was not telling her the truth, and Rachel wouldn't discover the lie until months later.

In June 1960, First Lady Jacqueline Kennedy invited her to serve on the Natural Resources Committee of the Democratic Advisory Council. Rachel Carson accepted the honor, on a limited basis. She wanted to do all she could, but she wanted to devote most of her time to her writing. Temporarily, she thought, she had health problems to overcome.

In the fall, she found out her health problems were not at all temporary. The tumor had not been benign. It was malignant, which meant that Rachel Carson had cancer. She immediately contacted Dr. George Crile, Jr., a physician at the Cleveland Clinic. He was a friend, and an expert on cancer treatments as well. Following his advice, she began radiation therapy.

To her editor, Paul Brooks, she wrote that the treatments would involve a "pretty serious diversion of time and capacity for work....But in the intervals I hope to work hard and productively. Perhaps even more than ever, I am eager to get the book done."

Rachel Carson near her home in Maine in 1961.

Rachel told just a few close friends that she had cancer, and told everyone else that she had arthritis. She worked as hard and as fast as she could, though at times she was virtually bedridden. She saw spring arrive from her bed. In March she wrote to a friend that she woke up one morning to the cries of migrating geese. She staggered to the window, calling out to little Roger to join her in the excitement. And then she went back to bed and worked on her manuscript.

The book began with a fable about a "silent spring"—a spring when no birds sang, no fish swam, and no bees buzzed about the flowers. During this strange and quiet spring, flowers turned brown, leaves fell off of trees, and children, as well as adults, came down with mysterious diseases and died. Rachel called it a silent spring because silence reigned over the land, as creatures large and small disappeared. After the fable, Carson explained clearly what would make the world die in such a grim manner. She wrote about the danger of pesticides in the food chain, and she alerted her readers to the alarming amount of chemicals in their lives.

Finally, in January 1962, Carson sent all but one chapter to her publishers in New York and to William Shawn, editor of the *New Yorker* magazine. Rachel hoped they would like what she had written, but even she did not realize how much this book meant to her. She did not know how important it had become to her that this book, even more than the others before it, be a good book. Then William Shawn called her to tell her it was terrific—she had done an excellent piece of work.

"Suddenly the tension of four years was broken," Rachel wrote to Dorothy Freeman, "and I let the tears come. I think I let you see last summer what my deeper feelings are about this when I said I could never again listen happily to a thrush song if I had not done all I could. And last night the thoughts of all the birds and other creatures and all the loveliness that is in nature came to me with such a surge of deep happiness that now I had done what I could—I had been able to complete it—now it had its own life..."

Silent Spring appeared in the *New Yorker* in a three-part short version beginning June 16, 1962. The book was published in September. Yet even before the magazine was printed or the book was seen on bookstore shelves, *Silent Spring* came under attack.

The American Medical Association, the Nutrition Foundation, and various chemical companies and associations spoke out against *Silent Spring*. In response to the book, the National Agricultural

Chemicals Association budgeted about $250,000 for a public relations campaign to improve the industry's image. Newspaper, television, and magazine editors were flooded with requests from the chemical industry to do stories about the benefits of pesticides. Many of the articles attacked Rachel Carson personally. They called her a food-faddist, nature nut, bird watcher, middle-aged Nervous Nellie, and worse.

Still, most members of the press sided with Rachel Carson. The *Saturday Review* said Carson presented the facts "sensibly." The reviewer applauded Carson for the courage she showed in writing a book on such a difficult and controversial subject. Stories alerting the public to the dangers of pesticides appeared in newspapers and magazines all across America. Alarmed readers wrote to newspapers wondering what was being done about the pesticide problems. Editors wrote columns, and reporters interviewed experts.

Other members of the press criticized Carson's book. *Time* magazine called *Silent Spring* "emotional and inaccurate." The review stated that scientists thought Carson's arguments were "unfair, one-sided, and hysterically overemphatic." *Reader's Digest* cancelled its contract to publish a short version of the book.

Still, Rachel Carson's mail told her that the American people supported her position. The mail at the Department of Agriculture was also strongly in support of Rachel Carson. The letters expressed "horror and amazement," one spokesperson told the *Saturday Review*. If pesticides were being used dangerously, many Americans wanted something done about them.

Though ill, Rachel Carson once more went on the road to promote her book. She made speeches, granted newspaper and magazine interviews, appeared at her *Silent Spring* publication party, attended luncheons and receptions in her honor, autographed copies of her book, and took part in a television debate on the subject.

Around her, the controversy swelled and surged. In all forms and in every publication they could find space in, representatives of the chemical industry attacked Rachel Carson. They questioned her scientific knowledge, they searched for errors in her book, and they called her names.

In a speech given in December 1962, to the Women's National Press Club, Rachel Carson finally responded to the attacks made on her. "One obvious way to try to weaken a cause is to discredit the person who champions it," she said. She also defended the central theory of her book, saying

her opponents were attacking statements she never
made. "Anyone who has really read the book
knows that I criticize the modern chemical method
not because it controls harmful insects but because
it controls them badly and inefficiently and creates
many dangerous side effects in doing so."

People were listening. President John F. Kennedy set up a committee to study the pesticides
issue. Rachel Carson met with the committee in
January 1963, and in May the committee issued a
report on its findings. It mentioned Rachel Carson.
"Until the publication of *Silent Spring* by Rachel
Carson, people were generally unaware of the toxi-
city of pesticides." Carson had alerted Americans,
and the world at large, to the dangers.

The report went on to recommend that the
government keep the public informed about the
dangers and problems of using pesticides, and also
about the value of chemicals that are used wisely
and safely. It said, "the use of pesticides must be
continued...[but] it has now become clear that...
while they destroy harmful insects and plants, pesticides may also be toxic to beneficial plants and animals, including man."

Rachel Carson had achieved her purpose. Now,
she wrote in a *New York Herald Tribune* article, it was
time to put these wise ideas into practice. Another

government committee was formed, this one a U.S. Senate committee that would study environmental hazards. Rachel Carson spoke to it, also, urging the senators to take action. "This is a problem," she said, "that must be solved in our time."

"You are the lady who started all this," said Senator Abe Ribicoff.

"She alerted us to the subtle dangers of 'An Age of Poisons,'" said U.S. Secretary of the Interior Stewart L. Udall. "She made us realize that we had allowed our fascination with chemicals to override our wisdom in their use."

All of Rachel Carson's books had brought her fame and awards, but *Silent Spring* won one that she valued most of all—the Schweitzer Medal of the Animal Welfare Institute. "I can think of no award that would have more meaning for me or that would touch me more deeply than this one, coupled as it is with the name of Albert Schweitzer," she said in her acceptance speech. "Dr. Schweitzer has told us that we are not being truly civilized if we concern ourselves only with the relation of man to man. What is important is the relation of man to all life..." Dr. Schweitzer, a 1952 Nobel Peace Prize winner, was known worldwide for his missionary work in Africa and for his concern for humankind.

Carson accepted the award in person, an act

which was becoming more and more difficult for her. The cancer in her body was advancing, though she was taking radiation treatment. Then, in the spring of 1963, she had a heart attack as well. Rachel did as much as she could. Still, she couldn't help regretting that she was unable to do so many of the things she wanted to do. She sent friends and colleagues in her place to give speeches and to accept honors and awards for her. "And all the opportunities to travel to foreign lands—all expenses paid—have to be passed up," she wrote to a friend.

That summer Jeanne Davis drove Rachel Carson, Roger, and their cat to Carson's seaside cottage in Maine. It was a quiet summer. Rachel took care of the house and Roger, but her heart was weakened, the cancer made movement difficult, and she had a painful case of arthritis as well. She often sat on her deck overlooking the ocean, her binoculars at her side, catching a passing glimpse of swooping birds, or of "wee beasts" going about their busy lives.

Carson spent restful afternoons with her neighbor and friend, Dorothy Freeman. Dorothy would read out loud, and Rachel would lie back on a picnic blanket watching the sky, the clouds, the gulls circling overhead, and the songbirds in the trees.

Sometimes she would talk about the scientific information she was reading, explaining it to Dorothy in clear, understandable language.

All too soon, the summer came to an end. One early fall morning, Rachel and Dorothy watched the fall migration of monarch butterflies. Later that day, Rachel wrote a note about the butterflies to Dorothy—"something I think I can write better than say...We talked a little about their [the monarch butterflies'] life history," Rachel wrote. "Did they return? We thought not; for most, at least, this was the closing journey of their lives."

It was a natural close to the butterflies' lives, and "it had been a happy spectacle," Carson wrote. "For ourselves," she added, comparing her own life to those butterflies' lives, "the thought is the same: when that intangible cycle has run its course it is a natural and not unhappy thing that a life comes to its end."

Rachel Carson thought this would be her last summer at the Maine cottage. She felt the illness in her body growing stronger while she grew weaker. Still, she managed a trip that fall to see the California redwoods, something she had always wanted to do. Her agent, Marie Rodell, went with her, and Rachel spent most of the time in a wheelchair. She gave a lecture at the Kaiser Medical Center in San

Francisco and then visited the Muir Woods.

That fall she was elected a member of the American Academy of Arts and Letters. This was a great honor, since the academy included just fifty members, all of them highly respected artists, writers, and musicians. In December Carson traveled to New York to accept the academy membership, and to receive the National Audubon Society's medal for achievement in conservation. She was also the guest of honor at an American Geographic Society dinner.

Rachel wrote to Dorothy Freeman "that now every month, every day, is precious." She felt that she had few left. Still, she thought she saw some improvement in her condition, and even began to hope that she might spend one more summer in Maine.

Yet she was not to see her beloved seacoast cottage again. Rachel Carson died on April 14, 1964. She asked that the last passage from *The Edge of the Sea* be read at her funeral.

Chapter / Ten

An urgent need to follow Rachel Carson's advice

Twenty-five years after publication of *Silent Spring*, Jay D. Hair, executive vice president of the National Wildlife Federation, reflects on what Rachel Carson has meant to the world.

"Rachel Carson's works, especially *Silent Spring*, are so eloquent, so carefully researched, and so prophetic that they have moved thousands of people from apathy to action," he says.

Once Rachel Carson had alerted the nation to the dangers of unsafe use of pesticides, change was quick to follow. Chemical companies, accustomed to doing business without anyone watching them, found themselves the object of intense scrutiny.

The United States Congress passed a number of major laws to control the use of chemicals and different forms of pollution. DDT was banned for most uses in the United States. Amendments to the Federal Insecticide, Fungicide, and Rodenticide Act (FIFRA) established regulations so that new pesticides would be tested for possible poisonous effects on creatures that live around the insects the pesticide is meant to control. The Clean Air Act was passed to help reduce air pollution, and the Clean Water Act to clean up water pollution. The Toxic Substances Control Act now sets rules for the manufacture of poisonous and dangerous substances; the Resource Conservation and Recovery Act sets rules for disposing of toxic substances; and the Superfund sets rules for cleaning up toxic materials in the environment. The Environmental Protection Agency (EPA) was formed to oversee the new environmental laws, and to make sure they were followed. The EPA is supposed to protect the environment, and the American people from harmful substances.

Americans are more aware today than ever before of the dangers posed by toxic chemicals and a great variety of pollutants. Citizens speak of air pollution, water pollution, toxic wastes, endangered species, and endangered wilderness areas. Students learn about acid rain—acidic pollution that travels with air currents and falls to the earth in rain and

This portrait bust of Rachel Carson, created by Una Hanbury, is displayed in the National Portrait Gallery.

snow—called "the silent spring of the 1980s" by
Massachusetts Governor Michael Dukakis. Newspapers print articles warning that some pesticides
can cause cancer. Still, pesticide runoff from agricultural areas and from urban areas pollutes rivers
and lakes. And Americans wash fruits and vegeta-
bles not to wash off farm dust, but to attempt to
remove pesticides that remain on the food.

"We are still not adequately protecting our
Earth from environmental assault," says Jay Hair.
"While the federal government has banned a handful of the most dangerous pesticides, more than
50,000 pesticide products are still on the market,
and less than 5 percent have been fully tested for
safety. The United States today produces one bil-
lion pounds of pesticides each year. Those fig-
ures alone illustrate that we haven't yet learned the
lesson that Rachel Carson so valiantly sought to
teach."

Michael McCloskey, of the Sierra Club, comments that the laws we have that are supposed
to control pesticide usage are not strong enough
and are not enforced well enough. "In the United
States, a considerable amount of progress has been
made in reducing the use of dangerous pesticides,"
says McCloskey. "However, DDT is still being
used widely around the world, and problems of the

unsafe use of pesticides have increased on a world-wide basis....There is an urgent need to follow Rachel Carson's advice to move away from the use of such pesticides toward more biological controls...and more farm interests in the United States are coming to realize that.''

The campaign for wise and thoughtful use of pesticides and other chemicals in this world—the campaign that Rachel Carson started with *Silent Spring*—continues.

Bibliography

Beebe, William. "Of and About the Sea." *Saturday Review* (27 December 1941).

Briggs, Shirley A. "A Decade After Silent Spring." *Friends Journal* (1 March 1972).

_____. "Remembering Rachel Carson." *American Forests* (July 1970).

_____. Telephone interview with author, 1987.

Brooks, Paul. "Courage of Rachel Carson." *Audubon* (January 1987).

_____. *The House of Life: Rachel Carson at Work.* Greenwich, CT: Fawcett Publications, Inc., 1972.

"Can human beings withstand the barrage of economic poisons?" *Consumer Bulletin* (October 1962).

Carson, Rachel. "A Battle in the Clouds." *St. Nicholas* (September 1918).

_____. *The Edge of the Sea.* Boston: Houghton Mifflin Company, 1955.

_____. "A Famous Sea-Fight." *St. Nicholas* (August 1919).

_____. "The Land Around Us." *New York Herald Tribune Sunday Magazine* (25 May 1952).

_____. Letter to Mary Frye, 22 February 1928.

_____. "A Message to the Front." *St. Nicholas* (February 1919).

_____. "Our Ever-Changing Shore." *Holiday* (July 1958).

_____. "Rachel Carson." *New York Herald Tribune Book Review* (7 October 1951).

_____. *The Sea Around Us.* 1950. Reprint. New York and Scarborough, Ontario: New American Library, Times Mirror, 1961.

_____. *Silent Spring.* 1962. Reprint. New York: Fawcett Crest, 1964.

_____. "A Story of the Sea." *St. Nicholas* (March 1919).

_____. *Under the Sea-Wind.* New York: Simon and Schuster, 1941.

_____. "Who I Am and Why I Came to PCW." College Essay, 1925.

_____. "A Young Hero." *St. Nicholas* (January 1919).

"Ecology: For Many a Spring." *Time* (24 April 1964).

Frisch, Bruce H. "Was Rachel Carson Right?" *Science Digest* (August 1964).

Gartner, Carol B. *Rachel Carson*. Literature and Life Series. New York: Frederick Ungar Publishing Co., 1983.

"The Gentle Storm." *Life* (12 October 1962).

Graham, Frank, Jr. "Rachel Carson." *EPA Journal* (November/December 1978).

_____. Since Silent Spring. Boston: Houghton Mifflin Co., 1970.

Harvey, Mary Kersey. "Using a Plague to Fight a a Plague." *Saturday Review* (29 September 1962).

Lear, John. "A Personality Portrait of Rachel Carson." *Saturday Review* (1 June 1963).

Leonard, Jonathon Norton. "—And His Wonders in the Deep." *New York Times Book Review* (1 July 1951).

"A Nation Troubled by Toxics." *National Wildlife* (February/March 1987).

"Pesticides: 'Action is Long Overdue'." *Colorado Wildlife* (May 1987).

Seif, Dorothy. Telephone interviews by author, 1987.

Sterling, Philip. *Sea and Earth, The life of Rachel Carson*. Women of America Series. New York: Thomas Y. Crowell Co., 1970.

Udall, Stewart L. "The Legacy of Rachel Carson." *Saturday Review* (16 May 1964).

Wareham, Wendy. "Rachel Carson's Early Years." *Carnegie* (November/December 1986).

Weis, Judith S. "Whatever happened to environmental policy?" *BioScience* (December 1986).

Whorton, James. *Before Silent Spring, Pesticides and Public Health in Pre-DDT America*. Princeton, NJ: Princeton University Press, 1974.

Williams, Ted. "'Silent Spring' Revisited." *Modern Maturity* (October/November 1987).

Index